WHEN I RETIRE, I WANT TO BE...

The 10-Step Retirement Possibility Journal

Karleen Tauszik

Published by Tip Top Books, Dunedin, Florida

Text and layout copyright © 2020 by Karleen Tauszik
Cover Illustration from BigstockPhoto.com, contributor AV Bitter
Cover Design Copyright © 2020 by Karleen Tauszik
Cover design and cover photo editing by Janet Tauszik

All rights reserved, including the right of reproduction in whole or in part in any form.

Summary: This journal provides people who are 55+ with a ten-step process to examine their talents, achievements, and past career experiences to better equip them for a successful and fulfilling transition into the retirement years.

ISBN: 978-0-9904899-7-9

Karleen Tauszik is an author, primarily of books for children ages 8-12. She has worked in Human Resources for over 15 years and she's passionate about helping people find the work they were meant to do. Visit her on the web at KarleenT.com, where you can see her other books and sign up for her newsletter.

> *If you don't know where you are going,*
> *you'll end up someplace else.*
>
> --YOGI BERRA

Are you nearing retirement age and wondering what you'll do during that next phase of life? Are you excited about retirement...or fearful? Do have things you've always wanted to do that you'd like to plan into your post-career years? Or maybe you're currently retired and are bored, unsure what to do next. If you're in any of these situations, this book is for you.

You're not alone. Most retirement books, articles, and seminars focus on your financial preparation for this phase of life. But few of them focus on your other riches: your talents, strengths, and interests. Many people who have not been happy in retirement aren't sure what their true talents are, and after years of being miserable in their jobs, they don't know how to make a better success of retirement. The result? Boredom, a lack of interest in life, and a greater focus on illness and limitations brought on by aging. This state of reduced productivity and contribution effects retirees mentally and physically as they surrender to the traditional concept of retirement model as a time to "take it easy".

That's why I wrote this book. With over fifteen years of Human Resources experience and as the author of three other "I Want To Be" career journals for various age groups, I realize the need for people to continue to use their true strengths and talents beyond the traditional working years.

"But I don't know my true strengths and talents," you might say. In this ten-step journal, you'll discover them. First, we'll explore your present situation—the reasons you bought this book and what you hope to achieve through it. Then we'll look back at your job history and the talents and interests you've had throughout your life. From there, we'll plan your future and look at how to apply your unique skills and talents to make the most of your retirement years.

If you work on one section a week, in just ten weeks you'll have a clearer direction for your next steps. And in the future, keep this book handy, refer back to it, and add memories and insights as they come to you. There are several pages at the end to record additional notes and ideas. Use *When I Retire, I Want To Be...* as your roadmap for retirement satisfaction and success.

Table of Contents

1. My Present Situation 1
2. Looking Back to Ages 6-12 5
3. Looking Back to Ages 13-18 7
4. Looking Back to Ages 19-22 11
5. My Career History to the Present 13
6. What My Adult History Tells Me 17
7. Life Analysis 19
8. My Ideal Life 23
9. My Ikigai 25
10. My Retirement Plan 29
Extra Pages for Notes and Ideas 33

1. My Present Situation

Before we explore your direction in retirement, let's assess your current situation.

The current date is _____ and you're interested in using this book because

When you look ahead ten years into your retirement, what do you think or feel about your future?

How does your current job (if you're still working) or your day-to-day retirement situation make you feel?

What things do you like about your current situation?

What do you dislike about your life right now? Are those aspects changeable?

_____

_____

_____

What are the factors that really drive your desire for change?

_____

_____

What impact do you feel you have on the world at this point? ☐ no real impact
☐ negligible impact ☐ negative impact ☐ positive impact ☐ great impact

What are your current hobbies?

_____

_____

What have you always wanted to learn more about?

_____

_____

How did your parents retire? What do you think were the pros and cons of that model?

_____

_____

_____

Did you (or do you) enjoy your career? Why or why not?

Does your vison of retirement include working or not? Because you need to financially or because you want to?

Other thoughts and insights about your situation at this point:

2. Looking Back to Ages 6-12

Looking back helps you move forward. It can give you insights into yourself which may have gotten buried over the years.

If you have a hard time recalling childhood memories, try asking your siblings, close relatives, and childhood friends. For more help jogging your memory, look at schoolwork, report cards, old family photos, and other memorabilia you or your parents kept from your childhood.

When adults asked you, "What do you want to be when you grow up?", what was your usual answer?

As a child, what were your favorite books usually about?

What were your favorite classes in elementary school?

What were your favorite collections and hobbies?

When you had free time, what did you like to do?

What was your favorite family vacation? Why?

When you were little, you were known as the kid who always

In your elementary school years, what was your proudest moment?

What were your top three talents or strengths during this period?

Additional memories that may be relevant are

3. Looking Back to Ages 13-18

This is an important time to explore because once you hit adolescence, chances are you started to get pulled away from your inborn strengths and talents. First, peer pressure was strong in pushing you away from childish things and into adulthood. That's normal and needed, but some of those childish things may have been keys to your future career success and overall satisfaction with life.

Also, during these years you became more aware of societal expectations and may have been pulled off track by well-meaning guidance counselors, teachers, mentors, and parents.

When you were in middle school and high school what career did you think you wanted to pursue? Why?

What were your favorite classes during these years?

Did you have a collection or a hobby during these years? What was it?

When you had free time, what did you like to do?

What extra-curricular activities were you involved in? Did you enjoy them, or were they forced upon you?

What did friends or family turn to you for help with?

Did you like working with others, or prefer solo projects?

As a teenager, what was your proudest accomplishment?

What was an event that really excited you? Why?

How do the answers in this section compare to your answers from ages 6-12? What changed? Why?

Did you start getting pushed or pulled in a certain career direction? How and by whom? Into what career possibilities?

Did you work or volunteer anywhere when you were old enough? List the jobs you had up until high school graduation if you had any. How did you get them? Why did you pursue those jobs? What parts were interesting or boring?

4. Looking Back to Ages 19-22

During these pivotal years after high school graduation, you likely felt pressure to make the "right" career decisions. Whether you went straight to full-time work after high school, pursued training for a trade, or went to college, these years started putting you more on track for the future.

Whether you went to college, pursued a technical training, or went straight into a job, why did you pick that major, trade, or profession?

Did you enjoy the studies, training, or job? If so, what was your favorite part? If not, what did you dislike?

Can you see a point here that catapulted you on to the right or wrong career path? Were these your decisions or were you steered by pressure from parents or societal expectations?

If you worked during these years, list the jobs you held. How did you get them? Why did you pursue those jobs? What parts were interesting or boring? Did they add to what you wanted for your future career?

5. My Career History to the Present

Now it's time to analyze your history as an adult. You'll think back over every job, volunteering commitment, or other major responsibility (such as full-time child raising or caretaking) since college graduation or since age 22 or 23. You'll look for some common threads of what you liked and what you didn't like. Insights like that will help you make better decisions going forward into retirement.

List every job or major responsibility up until the present. Then add notes on what you liked and didn't like, and how long you stayed in that situation. Why did you leave? Think about factors like your responsibilities, the environment you worked in, and the people you interacted with.

6. What My Adult History Tells Me

Review the last section. You might want to highlight some things that stood out to you. Refer to that section to answer these questions. They'll help you spot past missteps in your past choices, and help you make better decisions about your next moves into retirement.

Looking back at your adult experience, what are the top four or five things that made you happy in your work?

How many of those elements are in your present job or retirement situation, if any? Which ones?

Rate your experiences or jobs. Look back and pick your top favorite 3 and your least favorite 3.

Top 3:

Bottom 3:

Are there any common threads with the top 3 or the bottom 3? Why did you pick each one for that ranking?

Which jobs or experiences made time fly? Why?

Were any of your duties in line with the strengths you listed on page 6, your childhood strengths?

What has been your greatest accomplishment, in your opinion?

Additional things you noticed and want to note:

7. Life Analysis

You have unique strengths, but maybe you haven't been able to recognize them. After all, you've been living with them all these years and you might think they're common among most people. This section will help to highlight your unique talents.

Look back at pages 5 - 12 for ages 6 to 22. What did you want to be during those various phases?

From age 6 to 12:

From age 13 to 18:

From age 19 to 22:

Summarize your strengths and achievements from those younger years. Do you still feel strong in those areas?

Looking over the history of your jobs and experiences, what have been your smartest decisions?

More recently, what have you been happy about completing?

What gives you energy?

If you were to win first prize for anything, what would it be?

You can't pass up a book or article about

Friends and family tend to turn to you when they need help with

Ask at least five other people individually about what they see as your strengths. List the person and his/her response here.

If you've received any professional endorsements on Linked In, what talents and strengths did those people point out about you?

Now that you've answered these questions, what three words would you use to describe yourself? 1. 2.
3.

In your opinion, your top positive attributes are

Have those attributes been used in any of your jobs or experiences? How?

8. My Ideal Life

In this section, throw aside your reality and dream big. Think about your retirement life in an ideal world. Put on those rose-colored glasses while you consider these questions, and don't forget to include your strengths and positive attributes from the previous section. You just may find some nuggets here that can actually be incorporated into your retirement plans.

If you had an extra hour of free time, how would you spend it? What about a week of free time?

If you were going to start a business, it would be

What would you do if money were no object?

Your big retirement dream is

Your smaller retirement dreams are

Describe your ideal dream day in your retirement future. Where do you live? What type of work do you do, if any? What do you do in your spare time? What type of people do you hang out with? Do you travel? Where, and how often?

9. My Ikigai

Ikigai is a Japanese word that means, "a reason for living". According to this method, if you consider the factors that make life worthwhile—passion, mission, vocation, and profession—and find a path where all four overlap, you have found your best source of purpose and satisfaction.

As you can see from this illustration, your **mission** is the intersection of what you love and what the world needs. Your **vocation** is the intersection of what the world needs and what you can be paid for. Your **profession** is the intersection of what you do well and what you can be paid for. (Even if you no longer plan to work, you can still use this to find areas in which you can still contribute to society.) And your **passion** is at the intersection of what you do well and what you love to do. Finally, your **purpose** is at the intersection of all four circles.

In this model, if you can find something you love, which you are good at, which the world needs, and for which you can be paid, you've found your ideal direction for life, a direction that's a balance between the four forces. Whether you intend to work in retirement or not, reviewing these ikigai factors can give you clarity on your ideal life in this new phase of life. Take time over the next week to contemplate the answers to the questions in the four sections, using what you've learned about yourself from this journal. Write whatever answers come to mind. Try this for several days in a row, coming back to the questions and adding any new insights.

Things you can do that you love:

Things you can do that the world needs:

Things you can do which you can be paid for, if this is important to you in your retirement:

Things you can do that you're especially good at:

Have you found anything in your lists that is the same in all four sections?

Or have you found something that's the same in only three sections? Is there a way to make it four?

For example, if accounting is what you're good at and experienced in, and is what you can get paid for (if you want to continue earning money in retirement), and is something the world needs, is there a way it can bring you joy? What if you volunteered as an accountant for a non-profit that interests you? Or what if you started your own small accounting business?

Or if you love drawing cartoons and you're good at it, but you think no one would be interested in your work, is that true? There are others in the world getting publicity and payment for cartoons. How are they doing it? Can you research to find out?

Look back at page 17 at the four or five things that made you happy in your work. How many of them can be incorporated into your ideal retirement? How can you integrate them?

What about those interests from childhood and your teen years, on pages 5 through 10? Can you use any of those as you design your retirement plan?

Additional things you noticed and want to note:

10. My Retirement Plan

Congratulations! You've learned quite a bit about yourself, your past experiences, and your future potential by working through these 9 sections. Now it's time to set some goals for the next steps for your ideal retirement.

Over these past 9 chapters, what were the top things you learned?

Your ideal retirement opportunities are

Now set a target goal. You can't hit a target you can't see. Do you need to talk to a mentor or someone who can help you with the next steps? Or do you need to research your new opportunity or sign up for a class?

Your goal is to

A reasonable deadline is _____ .

It's important to get started while these ideas are fresh, even if it means you only take small steps. At least they'll be steps in the right direction. Remember, there's never a "perfect" time, so start now. Start moving toward this retirement goal.

Some steps you can take immediately are _____

_____

_____

_____

Your action steps over this month will be _____

_____

_____

_____

Looking ahead, your action steps next month will be _____

_____

_____

_____

Steps you'll need to take into the future will be _____

_____

_____

_____

Take inventory. What do you have already that will help you meet your goals? What do you need? Who can you ask for help?

Do you foresee some obstacles? Make a list of them here, along with ideas of how to deal with them.

As you consider new options for your future, think creatively. If you're still working, can you cut your hours at your present job to take on a part-time job in your ideal retirement profession? Can you start a side gig while still working, trying some of your ideas out? There are many possibilities on how to pivot toward your ideal retirement.

Good luck on your journey to optimizing your retirement by continuing to contribute and utilize your talents. Now that you know where you're going, you'll be able to more effectively map out how to get there. Keep this book handy as your guide, and you'll soon be sharing your best strengths with the world throughout your retirement years.

--- Notes & Ideas ---

--- Notes & Ideas ---

--- Notes & Ideas ---

--- Notes & Ideas ---

About the Author

Karleen Tauszik is the author of over 20 books. Most of them are for children ages 8 to 12. She created the popular career possibility journal for children, *When I Grow Up, I Want to Be…* and after hearing many adults say, "When are you going to write the book for adults?", she wrote this book, *When I Retire, I Want to Be…*, as well as *In My Next Job, I Want To Be* for mid-career people, and *When I Graduate, I Want To Be…* for ages 16 to 22.

Learn more by visiting Karleen's website at KarleenT.com. While you're there, keep up to date with her news and book releases by signing up for her newsletter.

www.ingramcontent.com/pod-product-compliance
Lightning Source LLC
Chambersburg PA
CBHW060428010526
44118CB00017B/2403